GW01605307

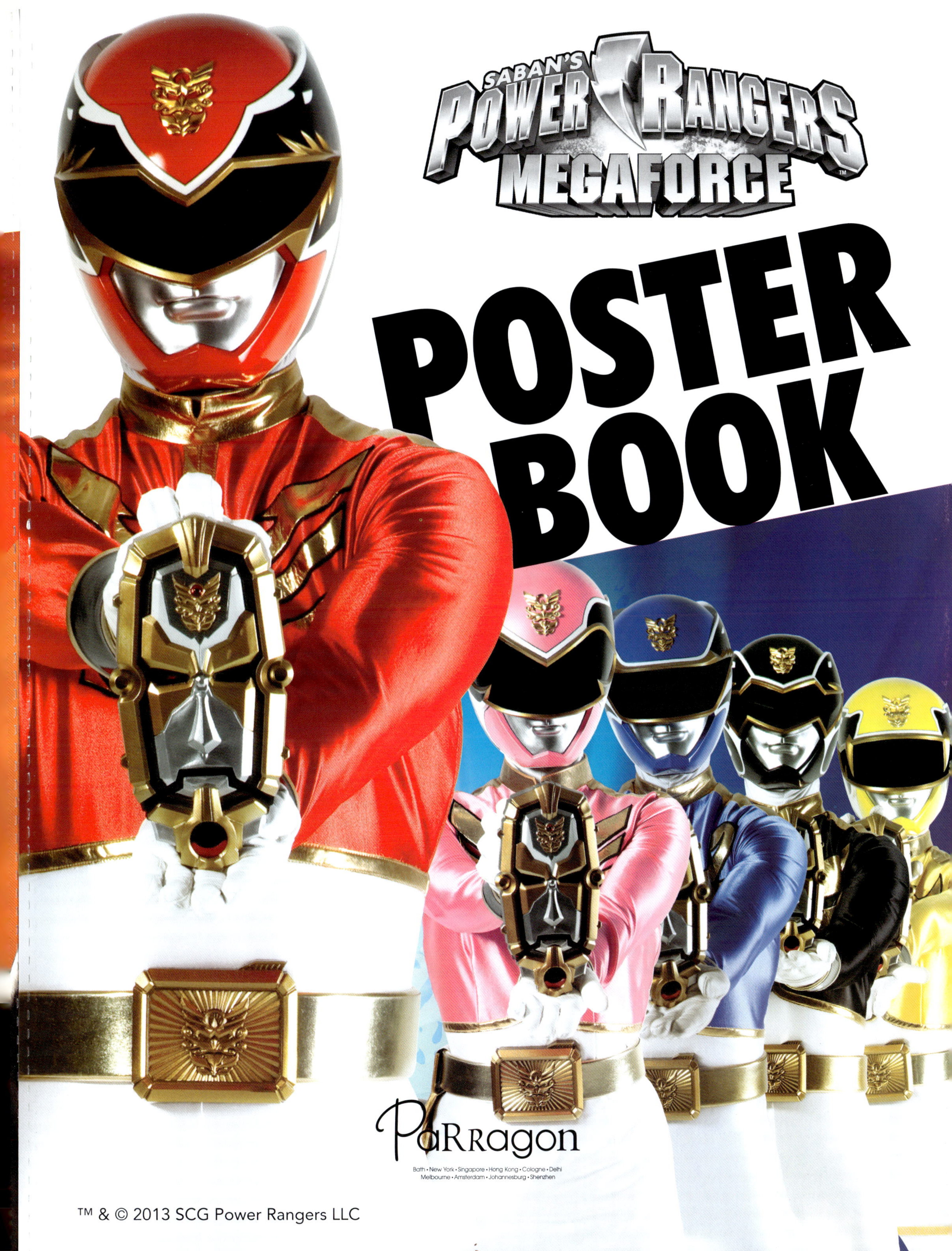
SABAN'S
POWER RANGERS
MEGAFORCE
™
POSTER
BOOK
Parragon
Bath • New York • Singapore • Hong Kong • Cologne • Delhi
Melbourne • Amsterdam • Johannesburg • Shenzhen

TROY

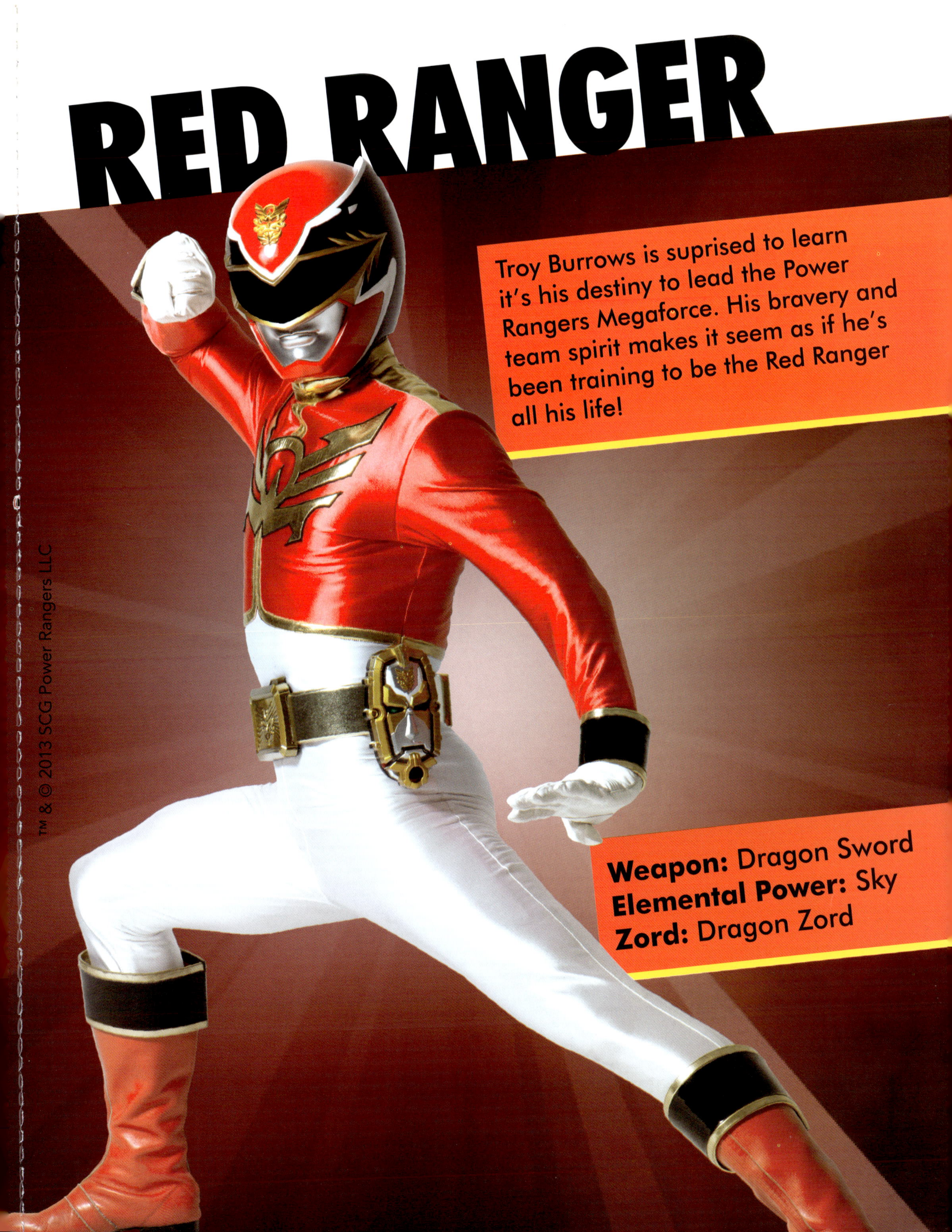
RED RANGER
Troy Burrows is suprised to learn
it's his destiny to lead the Power
Rangers Megaforce. His bravery and
team spirit makes it seem as if he's
been training to be the Red Ranger
all his life!
Weapon: Dragon Sword
Elemental Power: Sky
Zord: Dragon Zord

NOAH

BLUE RANGER

Although Noah isn't as strong as Jake and doesn't have Troy's martial-arts skills, he realizes his true strength is brainpower.

Weapon: Shark Bowgun
Elemental Power: Sea
Zord: Shark Zord

JAKE

BLACK RANGER

Jake sees his new superhero role as a chance to do great things, but he wishes that it didn't have to be a secret! Jake is a great addition to the Megaforce team.

Weapon: Snake Axe
Elemental Power: Earth
Zord: Snake Zord

KNIGHT DYNAMIC!